thınkterior

Amazing Bespoke Kids Interiors

Visual Profile Books, New York

Published by:
Visual Profile Books, Inc.
389 Fifth Avenue, New York, NY 10016
Phone: 212.279.7000
www.visualprofilebooks.com

Distributed by:
National Book Networks, Inc.
15200 NBN Way, Blue Ridge Summit, PA 17214
Toll Free (U.S.): 800.462.6420
Toll Free Fax (U.S.): 800.338.4550
Email orders or Inquires: customercare@nbnbooks.com

ISBN 13: 978-0-9834501-3-9
ISBN 10: 0-9834501-3-7

Library of Congress Cataloging in Publication Data:
Amazing Bespoke Kids Interiors

Table of Contents

"Every child is an artist. The problem is how we remain an artist when we grow up."

— Pablo Picasso

At Thinkterior Studio we produce
imaginatively designed spaces for
hotels and private homes.

We work directly with our clients from
concept through to manufacturing and install
to create totally unique spaces for children.

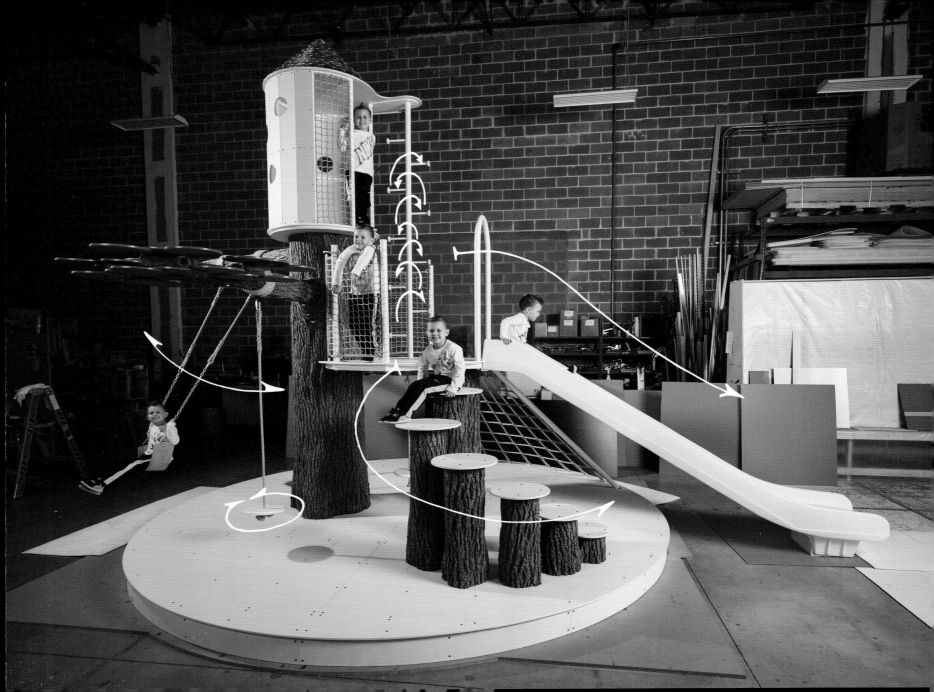

Introduction

Amazing Spaces for Amazing Kids

Every child knows there are places where only children can go. They may be beckoning in the nearest closet or hiding in make-believe worlds, but they are as real as a child's imagination. No boy or girl would doubt the existence of the tree house described by Sheldon ("Shel") Silverstein in his 1974 classic book of children's poetry, Where the Sidewalk Ends: "A tree house, a free house,/A secret you and me house,/A high up in the leafy branches/Cozy as can be house." Unfortunately, most children will never have a tree house. But what if one could actually be designed, built and visited every day? This is the mission of Thinkterior, a design firm devoted to designing, fabricating and installing unique, custom-made environments for children--just as children might imagine them.

Thinkterior co-founder Chris Jones began creating environments for children purely for fun. A childhood passion for making things led him to study art and design at West Virginia University, where he earned a BFA in graphic design. After years spent managing corporate identity programs for clients large and small, he embarked on a do-it-yourself home improvement project that would change his career, designing and building a special bedroom for his son. Not only did the attractive and playful space delight his little boy, it attracted the attention of neighbors and friends. An initial request to make something equally magical for another child resulted in another request--and another. In 2013, Chris decided to devote himself entirely to producing what he likes to call "amazing Bespoke Kids Interiors for amazing kids."

In the pages of Thinkterior: Amazing Bespoke Kids Interiors readers can peer inside some of the choicest private projects Chris and his firm have completed for families in the United States, Europe, Asia, Latin America and the Middle East. Children of all ages will be intrigued by such one-of-a-kind sights as a magic tree house, a royal, carriage-shaped crib, an enchanted fairyland forest, and a fun-filled clubhouse and loft—each one crafted from scratch--that can actually be entered, touched and explored. In fact, it is likely that the happy visitors to these Bespoke Kids Interiors wisely disregard age limits of any kind. As George Bernard Shaw pointed out, "We don't stop playing because we grow old; we grow old because we stop playing."

Creating magic is hard work

The business that began as a home improvement project became Thinkterior in 2015. Chris, the new firm's co-founder and creative director, joined forces with co-founding partners Matt Thorpe, marketing director, and Anthony Hughes, production director, to develop bedrooms, playrooms and other dedicated spaces for children in North America, Europe, the Middle East and Asia, with an obvious emphasis on the United States, where Chris is based in Virginia, USA and Asia, where Matt is based in Singapore and Tony is based in Bangkok, Thailand. All three are devoted fathers of children ranging in age from two to thirteen years, share a passion for great design, and relish the challenge of making dreams come true for families around the world.

"We don't stop playing because we grow old; we grow old because we stop playing."
– George Bernard Shaw

Creating magical settings for budding princesses, buccaneers, astronauts and other little people requires considerable adult effort, to be sure. "Our goal is to make families happy," Chris declares. "Many families respond to our presentations by saying 'Yes, yes, yes.' But they often change specific details. We do everything possible to give them what they want." The development process begins when Thinkterior interviews a family to determine its hopes, budget and timetable, as well as the dimensions of the spaces to be transformed. Next comes a full design, including custom furniture, color palettes, accessories and other architectural elements, that the family can review and alter before the design is finalized with artistic renderings and scaled drawings. Once everything is approved by the family, Thinkterior fabricates all the furniture and architectural elements, ships them to the job site, and installs them with the participation of skilled local craftsmen and builders.

Ideally, the family has retained an architect who will work with Thinkterior. In the absence of an architect, Chris and his colleagues routinely plan with contingencies. "You must always expect the unexpected, especially overseas," he cautions. "Walls are seldom plumb or square. You bring multiple types of fasteners because the construction could be made of anything. Local materials and tools may not serve our purposes. Metric conversions can be confusing."

Each Thinkterior project is founded on functional design, unfettered imagination, quality materials and workmanship, and uncompromised product safety, following U.S. standards, the strictest in the world. To ensure that Bespoke Kids Interiors embody the latest thinking about ergonomics and safety, Thinkterior continuously monitors regulations and research from government agencies, businesses and academia in order to incorporate them into its own company handbook. "Whether

we're dealing with children's heights and weights, handrails or crib safety," Chris admits, "we leave nothing to chance." This commitment is especially pertinent for Thinkterior, whose singular environments shun standardized components—except for its innovative myWall, a modular, wall-mounted storage system designed to be customized, adapted and re-used as children grow and their needs change.

How to assemble a dream

Chris and his colleagues have proudly designed, fabricated and installed most if not all Bespoke Kids Interiors for families in what amount to turnkey projects, giving them maximum control over their work. This remains Thinkterior's preferred modus operandi. Of course, the firm's expanding outreach to families worldwide has necessitated introducing other options. Now, in addition to offering turnkey service, Thinkterior can also design a

space and fabricate its furniture and architectural elements to be shipped and installed by others, or simply design projects for others to fabricate and install. "I continue to believe the best outcomes for our clients come from letting us do everything," Chris understandably maintains.

He expects to keep project design and fabrication in the United States, at least for the foreseeable future. Yet the day will probably arrive when Thinkterior delegates much of the work to others. That's the price of success. Not surprisingly, Chris hopes families will let his firm do everything. After all, Walt Disney, who built an entertainment empire based on stimulating the imagination of children everywhere, liked to insist, "If you can dream it, you can do it."

If the following pages are any indication, Thinkterior is dreaming it and doing it as hard as it can.

Inspired by kids, created by dads

Thinkterior has been created by three dads with a passion for great design. We also have a bunch of kids ranging from two to thirteen years old who are our biggest source of inspiration when creating Thinkterior products.

We understand a child's bedroom is much more than just a place to sleep. It's a fort, a spaceship, a jungle or a café in the heart of Paris. It's also a place to learn, a place to be entertained and a place to "be me."

At Thinkterior we view a child's room as an ecosystem, a place where a boy or girl evolves and interacts with the things around him or her.

At the heart of the Thinkterior ecosystem is myWall, a premium hardwood panel system that allows furniture, storage and toys to "plug and play" through a secure locking system.

Thinkterior believes a child's bedroom should evolve over time. Through our products, we help children from toddlers to teenagers in creating their own perfect spaces.

Chris Jones
Creative Director

Anthony Hughes
Production Director

Matt Thorpe
Marketing Director

We
Thinkterior
Differently!

We are much more than "an interiors company." Thinkterior Studio works closely with families to create the ultimate room for every child. We operate on a one-to-one level with them, developing design briefs, selecting materials, producing comprehensive designs and fabricating all components to ensure that each family gets the finest furniture and fittings, as well as a unique design that reflects the personality of their child. Our studio's philosophy is simple:

Each concept we create incorporates the following elements: fun, adventure, creativity and excitement.

This approach, combined with high quality materials, craftsmanship and strict safety guidelines, guarantees that your child's room will perfectly match his or her character.

FAIRY LAND

THEME Every element of this room evokes images from the Enchanted Forest. Tiny lights twinkle like fireflies, curtains swing from real tree limbs, and sticker stones lay a pathway to the bed. Ceramic mushrooms and birdhouses are scattered throughout the room, creating perfect hiding spots for fairies, pixies and other magical friends. The dominant color of both bedroom and bathroom—a soft, feminine pink—creates a soothing, yet wondrous atmosphere. In the corner sits a large tree with a child-size door at the base, promising a child-size adventure on the other side.

FOCUS Illuminated by two beautiful flower-shaped lamps, the six-foot-diameter circular bed becomes the centerpiece of the room. Imitation bark on the bed's exterior augments the room's theme and makes it easy for a child to believe she has stepped out of the suburbs and into the forest. Three lily pads extending from tree bark serve as both steps to the bed and stools to sit on. Ready-made for princess parties and sleepovers, the bed easily accommodates two to three small children or an adult. Twelve- foot ceilings enhance the sense of openness, while soft

lighting and comfy pillows make this a cozy reading and resting spot.

STORAGE The shelves on the rear of the bed and the two compartments in the tree—one covered by a double-door, the other by a miniature door— supplement the storage capacity of the room's giant closet without interrupting the theme.

GROWTH The bed meets standard specifications for a baby crib, and can accommodate both children and adults. The railing is easily removed when the baby girl becomes a "big girl," and eventually, a teenager.

SAFETY Rounded edges on all of the room's furnishings help prevent nasty bumps, and lamps are positioned well out of reach of small children. The mattress is designed to fit snugly to meet current crib safety standards, while a 26-inch railing allows this bed to act as a safe, comfortable and fun play area.

Bed mattress is 1830mm (6 feet) in diameter. Fabricated with safety specifications for an infant.

— Chris Jones, Thinkterior

MAGIC TREE HOUSE

THEME Inspired by the Magic Tree House series of children's books from Random House, this indoor tree house provides entertainment, fun and a place for children to read about or imagine adventures through time. A blue sky, green meadows, and distant matching beech trees recreate the magic of Jack and Annie's Frog Creek, and help bring the characters from the series to life.

FOCUS An armoire, ceiling swing and climbing rope give the structure a true tree house look and feel. A drop-down drawing and writing table, wheeled work table and recessed ceiling lights equip the room for more than play. The tree house has electric interior lighting, a window to the outdoors and a playful sliding shutter over a window to the room. The armoire forms a raised, nine-foot-wide play area, while a TV within one of the wall's floor-to-ceiling cabinets—with a delightful sliding ladder—transforms the room into a family theater perfect for watching movies and holding Wii competitions.

STORAGE The bottom of the drawing table is a magnetic chalk board that doubles as a display for children's art works. The tree's small niches are for parents' shoes; the large compartment stores children's shoes and school bags. Books, games, toys, DVDs, Wii and other computer accessories are stored in the wall cabinets. The armoire contains two spacious drawers and four nifty hinged storage bins. A rack of handy "vegetable buckets" above the armoire stores crayons, scissors and other useful items.

GROWTH The room easily adapts from playroom to party room, study room and even bedroom, as the tree house easily accommodates a twin-size mattress.

SAFETY The rungs and rails of the ladder, as well as the grab bars beside the tree house door, are wrapped with easy-to-grip rope for safe climbing. The drawing table has spring-loaded hinges to help prevent it from dropping accidentally from the wall, and the table door has double sets of locks up top for safety. The interior of each storage compartment is carpeted just as the tree house floor is to provide extra padding.

The floordrobe contained more than 44 square feet (13,411 mm) of cubic floor storage space.

— Chris Jones, Thinkterior

SLEEP BABY SLEEP

THEME Created for a baby girl, this room is magical, feminine and very pink. At its heart is the Carriage Crib, surrounded by a large oak tree with adorable animals, baby blocks, a cozy window seat and an upholstered play area on the floor.

FOCUS The compelling size and detail of the Carriage Crib, with a dainty canopy held in place by woodland creatures, immediately catches a visitor's attention, and is enhanced by the piece's fascinating colors and textures. Wall murals, fabrics, accent furniture and lighting accent the beauty of the crib. A handsome Dutch door with a child-size myDoor entrance lets this princess feel at home as soon as she steps in the room.

STORAGE The room has closet organizers for everyday items, and cubicle storage is discreetly hidden behind the wall-mounted letter blocks.

GROWTH As the room's occupant grows from baby to toddler to child and 'tween, the room will be easily transformed with age-appropriate toys, pictures, bedding and fabrics. The crib portion of the carriage can be removed and fitted with a larger mattress, saving both time and money in the future. Letter blocks are easily updated by simply removing the letters and replacing them with mirrors or panels bearing bright colors or descriptive images.

SAFETY Standard precautions are taken to secure power outlets and keep exposed shelving out of reach. Thickly padded upholstered squares featuring colors and patterns that coordinate with the fabrics on the window seat and valance create a visually inviting, comfortable and safe place to play.

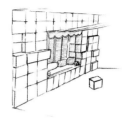

Because the carpet brings the entire room together, I was determined to make the floor squares perfect. I cut 200 pieces of carpet padding and custom carpet pieces, arranged the design appropriately, and fit them snugly onto the floor to create the illusion of a rug.

— Chris Jones, Thinkterior

"Sleep baby. Sleep, sleep, sleep…"

– Mantra of new parents everywhere

ACTION JACKSON

THEME The main theme for this room is an active, physical and personalized experience for a growing boy. This is achieved with the use of bold colors, creative inclusion of personal favorites and the use of industrial materials.

FOCUS The main focus of the room is the 12-foot long x 4-foot wide elevated bed. The bed is the focal point of the room and leaves ample space for activity within the room beneath. A secondary focus of the room is the desk, positioned in a private corner of the room, outfitted with custom lighting and a suspended desktop designed to support growing technical needs and school assignments.

STORAGE A large armoire stands at the far end of the room between the bed and wall. The armoire has eight separate storage units that are approximately 12 inches high x 24 inches wide by 8 inches deep. These enclosed storage spaces are convenient for anything a growing boy may need to put away and convenient enough to make cleaning up easy for him. At the far corner of the room, a chair and built-in desk offer a convenient outlet for serious play or work.

GROWTH The room is designed for active children ages 8 to 18. There are three ways for children to enter the bed: climbing the knotted rope, scaling the custom rock wall or gripping the pipe monkey bars mounted on the wall and along the ceiling. (The ladder is only for parents.) While these are the intended ways to enter the bed, they are also a convenient safety system to prevent younger siblings from getting into the boy's private things.

SAFETY Although this room is designed for an older child, safety is still a critical element, so every detail in the room has been reviewed for safety. The raised bed includes extra long and high side boards, ensuring that any rolling in bed is kept safe. The decking is sanded and edges have been cleaned to prevent any potential splintering. Power outlets are covered using exterior industrial outlets for the switches and plugs, which also looks really cool.

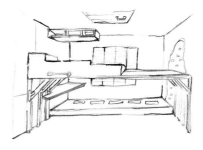

440 license plates across the ceiling take up some serious time.

— Chris Jones, Thinkterior

CLUBHOUSE

THEME The overall theme for this boys' space is a functional, family-friendly escape where time spent together or alone is comfortable and exciting. The integration of the work space, clubhouse and family entertainment area creates an environment that brings the whole family together in projects, recreation and relaxation. Each element works harmoniously with others, merging the creative and functional components into the perfect family escape.

FOCUS The two-story clubhouse is the focal point of the large space and simultaneously separates and blends the room's distinct neighborhoods. The clubhouse has an upper level loft overlooking the main room and a lower enclosed space with windows looking out into the playroom and work room. Because expenses were critical for this project, the use of many Ikea products helped to keep the fabrication and construction costs within budget.

STORAGE Storage is abundant on the walls, in the cabinets and even beneath the floor. The massive built-in cabinets house the television and gaming consoles, and the custom designed peg walls accommodate additional shelving that can be continually modified to accommodate new or shifting passions. While the raised floor provides the base for the clubhouse and fort, the flush mounted floor pieces can be pulled up to reveal large, open storage volumes perfect for toys to be brushed into hiding.

GROWTH The entire space is designed to be always fun--and never outgrown. The clubhouse and loft will remain a focus for the family's boys for years, and the media area will draw the family together whether the featured program is a favorite animated movie or the newest adventure series. The adjoining workroom and its moving storage table provide the perfect arts and crafts area, and are well suited for future homework and science fair projects.

SAFETY The boys' desire to climb, jump, run, and swing is encouraged in this great space, and the attention to detail ensures that they will be safe. From the strong cargo netting enclosing the upper level of the clubhouse to the added care taken with the lumber to impart a soft clean feel without splintering--plus the extra wide borders in the flush mounted floor storage--this space gives its family a fun and safe space.

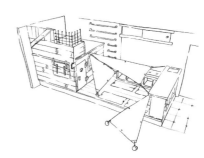

This area combined three of my favorite elements--floor armoire, fort canopies, and peg walls.

— Chris Jones, Thinkterior

ONCE UPON A TIME

An unusual and exceptionally beautiful work of art, the Carriage Crib, like the carriages of old it is modeled after, transports children to a time and place where prancing white horses, flowing gowns, and suits of armor are commonplace. The crib cleverly holds a standard round mattress that is perfect for sleeping as well as for transporting Cinderella to the ball. The carriage, wheels, balustrades and trim are painted different colors and accented by custom fabrics for the crib cover and pillows. A variety of accessories, including a colorful, fringed canopy and an assortment of pillows outfit the Carriage Crib to enhance fairytale themes and bedroom designs for both boys and girls.

SAFETY A sturdy railing meets current crib safety standards and encloses the crib to prevent babies and small children from falling out. Edges are rounded, and wheels are immobile so the carriage remains stationary. The entire railing is removable so the child can graduate to using the carriage as a bed with a toddler mattress.

STORAGE The rear suitcase box is used for both storage and as a changing table. A standard changing pad fits perfectly on the top.

Creating a design that worked for both a round crib as well as a toddler mattress insert was a challenge. To make it work, I had to make the frame of the carriage thin enough to fit the round crib setup, but at the same time, wide enough to manage a toddler mattress insert.

— Chris Jones, Thinkterior

"They say if you dream a thing more than once, it's sure to come true."

– Brianr Rose, Sleeping Beauty

THE COBBLER

THEME Every element of this room is tied to a traditional nursery rhyme. From the "Old Woman Who Lived in a Shoe" to "Hickory Dickory Dock," the Cobbler brings to life some of childhood's most memorable and endearing rhymes.

FOCUS To counter the room's high ceiling, the design introduces elements with both comparable height and considerable warmth, making the room feel spacious, yet cozy. A large, shoe-shaped armoire pays homage to the "Old Woman" and is built in place from floor to ceiling. It features curtained doors and drawer fronts, a wooden shingle roof with a blue bird on top, and a clothesline for baby's favorite wares. The mural over the crib, showing the Cow Jumping over the Moon and her counterpart, the Dish Running Away with the Spoon, adds fantasy and humor. Quaint, hand-painted stone walls that surround the shoe and hardwood flooring that partially replaces wall-to-wall carpeting help unify the room. An organic curve unites the wood and carpet gracefully, adding visual interest and organic beauty.

STORAGE The shoe holds clothing and linens, while the changing table stores diapers and diaper accessories. Shelving installed above the changing table adds color and interest, while creating room for stuffed animals, pictures, toys and treasures.

GROWTH The room's childlike theme and magical giant shoe, although intended for young children, are sufficiently functional and artistic to remain an endearing attraction for the room's occupant throughout childhood and adolescence.

SAFETY Precautions are taken to secure power outlets, keep exposed shelving out of reach of little hands, and allow medicinal items to be secured in a safe, convenient location. The clothesline is suspended high above the room and is secured to stay out of reach.

The inner frame of the shoe proved to be the most complicated part of this build. I created a scale model showing the full interior structure to make the overall construction easier.

— Chris Jones, Thinkterior

Tiny Yawn
and Slee
Nurser

and

MYWALL® PLAY

THEME myWall® Play uses the myWall® Ecosystem, an interchangeable set of furniture components that supports play, storage and work. Its modular nature means that myWall® Play grows with the needs of the child, from toddler to teen and beyond. The myWall® system provides parents flexible storage and play options, even when floor space is limited. Think of it as "vertical play," taking toys and activities off the floor and onto the wall.

FOCUS A child's bedroom is much more than a space to sleep. It is a place to play, learn and discover that our modular play system enhances, using plug-and-play accessories that cater to children of all ages. As screen time increasingly competes with "imagination time," our games and toys help to address the balance, making a child's bedroom a place where fun, adventure and learning can be experienced directly. Our toys are specifically designed to nurture cognitive skills, spatial awareness and hand-eye coordination in a fun and imaginative way. Vertical play also makes playtime more active, increasing mobility by encouraging a child to keep moving--standing up, walking and even climbing.

GROWTH The modular nature of the myWall® Ecosystem allows the myWall® Play accessories to be height adjusted, so the wall can grow up with the child. Parents can add age-appropriate toys and accessories to the wall to meet their child's latest developmental needs. With a wide range of accessories for multiple age groups and the ability to use the myWall® system for study and storage, the product can last from childhood to adulthood.

SAFETY We take safety very seriously in all our products and installations. The myWall® Ecosystem, made from renewable hardwood, is strong and durable. The fastening system employs lateral down force to make base panels extremely stable, and the locking pins result in very secure fittings. We only use non-toxic paint for our panels and accessories, and minimize the use of small parts in the assembly of our products. All myWall® Play products are easy to wipe clean and are machine washable.

BEST of year
FINALIST 2017

INTERIOR DESIGN

AdaptivDC is the current resource to commercial designers, retailers, offices and schools for myWall in the United States.

www.adaptivdc.com

"Play is our brain's favorite way of learning."

— Chris Jones, Thinkterior

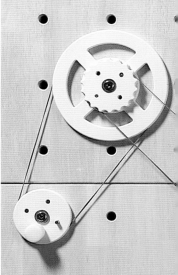

MYDOOR

THEME Too often the door to a room is taken for granted or ignored altogether. However, the entrance into a space can be as creative and fun as the space itself. Installing myDoor, with its separate openings for children and adults, brings imagination, function and personalized charm to any room design, whether the room beyond is a whimsical forest or outer space. It can be integrated into any room design or existing space to introduce a personalized bespoke feel, enhance the existing theme, and dramatize the act of entering or leaving the room.

FOCUS myDoor immediately becomes a focal point in any room, drawing the attention of adults and children alike with the promise of adventure on the other side. Children will be drawn to the door scaled perfectly for them, fostering a sense of independence, ownership and excitement. Adults will probably respond to myDoor with an intense longing to be younger and smaller again.

GROWTH myDoor offers a unique and safe way for smaller children to enjoy access to spaces in a way that builds their independence and confidence. They will grow taller than the door entrance long before they outgrow the desire to use it.

"Open the door to a child's imagination."

— Chris Jones, Thinkterior

GIDDY UP

THEME At some point, every little boy imagines himself a cowboy riding horseback, herding cattle over the plains and confronting ferocious outlaws. High noon or not, the Wild West is brought to life in this room with fantastic detail, thanks to a Chuck Wagon bed, Western-style drawers and a variety of room accents.

FOCUS The room's central feature is the Chuck Wagon bed, a companion to the signature Princess bed in our Kidtropolis project. Replicating a chuck wagon in every aspect, this version of Old West transport comes complete with wagon wheels, a canvas canopy and a ladder. Accessories such as a frying pan, lantern, bucket, rope and milk barrel set the stage for life on the range, while pictures of cowboys, Indians, teepees, campfires and ten-gallon hats evoke images of the OK Corral. Plush toy horses, a small wagon and a pup tent add finishing touches to the atmosphere.

STORAGE The wagon's front high seat serves as a changing table complete with pad. Convenient storage areas are located in the back and the side box.

GROWTH The Chuck Wagon bed works as a baby crib and is suitable for a toddler up to the age of four.

SAFETY A safety railing around the walls of the bed prevent the baby from falling out, and can be removed when needed. Wheels and accessories are immobile to guarantee that the wagon is safe for rest and play.

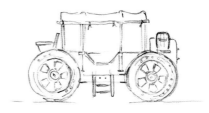

This bed is created on the same frame as my carriage crib bed.

— Chris Jones, Thinkterior

"Cowboys rock."

–Finn K., age 5

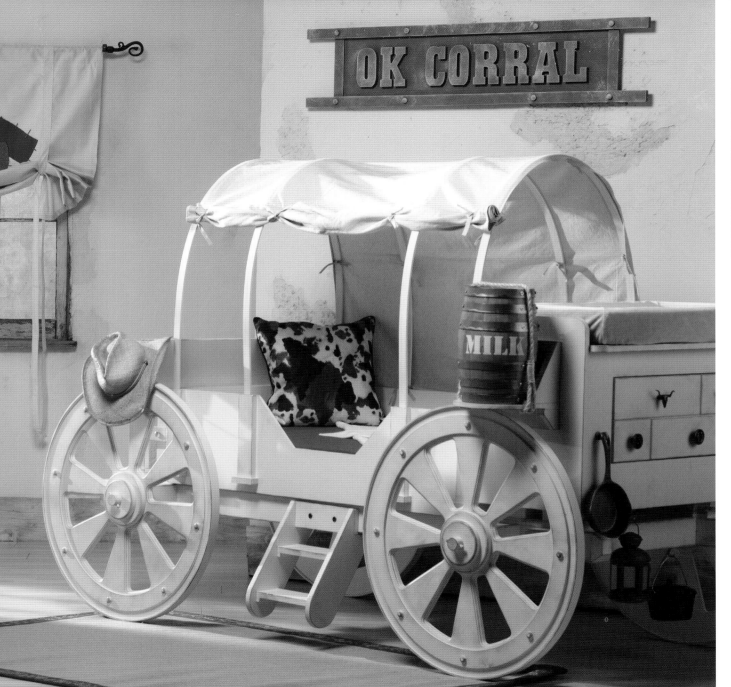
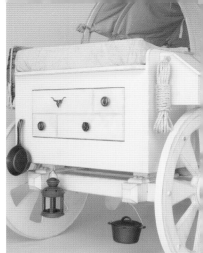

BURTON CHAIR

THEME Our client wanted to create a totally unique and inspired chair to accompany their equally unique and gifted son from his toddler to his 'tween years. They requested that the chair be a multifunctional piece they could convert from a high chair to a study chair, and to look as if it had been pulled straight from a Tim Burton film.

FOCUS The initial focus of the piece was on the elements it had to incorporate. Some elements are creative, some are functional and some are personal. The most visible features include the exaggerated height, removable light fixture, adjustability for multiple ages, storage for books and toys, and distinctive casters for easy mobility.

STORAGE The piece is designed with multiple storage options to house all the creativity a little boy can imagine. Each of the books forming the base of the seat has pull-out spines revealing storage areas perfect for books, sketch pads and small toys. Additional storage is concealed in secret compartments in the armrests, ideal for pencils or crayons.

GROWTH Whimsical as the piece is, it has been carefully designed to evolve with the little boy. The seat goes up and down over a 12-inch span, which should keep up with him as he grows. The colors incorporated into the piece are derived directly from the family's home, and will compliment the new setting.

SAFETY Safety is a primary concern for any furniture that we build, and this chair is no exception. The essential intent of the chair is to be a venue where the little boy can eat, learn, play and create, so it must keep him safe and secure during all these activities. For his early years a security harness system is installed to protect him from falling. The harness system can adapt as he grows, reducing to just a lap belt with belts that can be removed altogether when he no longer needs them.

A full-scale model of the chair was created with brown cardboard in order to work out the exact scale of elements.

— Chris Jones, Thinkterior

MERRY-GO-ROUND

THEME The sheer delight of the merry-go-round—an enduring symbol of childhood—is captured in this beautiful room paying homage to the carousel. The ageless joy and beauty of a classic carousel creates a magical space where anything seems possible.

FOCUS Designed for two special twins, the carousel stands almost 14 feet tall and eight and a half feet wide to hold two baby cribs. Two hand-painted carousel horses (whose images are reproduced in framed photos above the changing tables) complete the authentic look. Window treatments start at the center of the carousel with fabric that arches out to each window to pull together the entire room. Custom fabrics are used throughout the space, and the trapdoor entrance to the attic within the room is disguised as an oversized, vintage amusement park ticket. A wall-mounted television is framed with a monkey on top to ensure that even modern items have a vintage feel.

STORAGE An 18-foot by 12-foot wall of letter blocks creates an abstract armoire that provides storage for clothes, toys, books and other items. The center blocks create a bench seat along the wall, while freestanding blocks within the room help add to the illusion that all of the blocks in the room are actually stacked.

GROWTH The wall armoire can be easily updated to accommodate growing children by removing the letters and repainting the blocks in another style.

SAFETY Everything in the room is secure. If accidental falls or slips do occur, the floor has been custom made to be soft and safe. Two-foot-square floor pads created with medium density fiberboard and two layers of carpet padding topped with fabric cover the floor to create the feel of walking on pillows.

Since this is such a large build, installation was a challenge — especially since the only entryway is via a stairwell. Many pieces had to be created in parts and later assembled within the room.

— Chris Jones, Thinkterior

INIALA BEACH HOUSE

THEME The overall brief for the Iniala Beach House, a luxury beach resort in Phuket, Thailand, was to create what the owner described as "my perfect hotel." Each room would be different, embodying the very best in contemporary art and design. As part of his strategy, the owner wanted a special place for children offering considerably more than a generic Kids Club with a few activities and a PlayStation.

FOCUS The brief given to Thinkterior's Chris Jones was to produce a "totally immersive vacation experience for children" ages 3 to 13 years, where every day at the Iniala Kids Hotel would be a new adventure. For the junior guests lucky enough to vacation on the Island of Iniala, the guest experience starts when they are met by one of five dedicated Kids Hotel staff and check into their own Kids Hotel room. Each child gets a specially designed backpack full of goodies, including a hardback book that sets out his or her adventures during the family's stay. Children have a choice of sleeping in a tree house or a cave, and share a story around a "camp fire" each evening that sets up the next day's activities.

GROWTH Within their own dedicated space, junior guests can play, eat and sleep as well as get involved with such activities as cooking classes, treasure hunts or even staging a show for their parents at the built-in theater.

SAFETY Iniala Kids Hotel delivers junior guests a genuine, four-star experience, guaranteeing them the "best holiday ever" in adventures that are both exciting and safe, while their parents get some serious relaxation at the impressive main property.

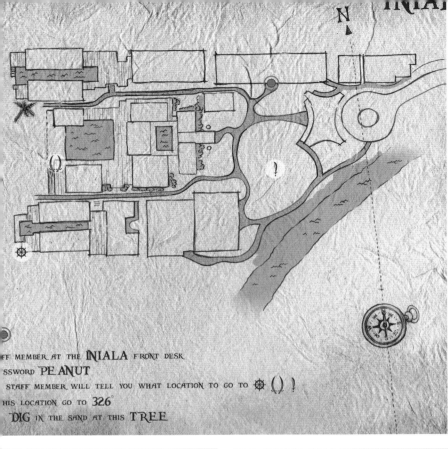

FF MEMBER AT THE **INIALA** FRONT DESK

SSWORD **PEANUT**

STAFF MEMBER WILL TELL YOU WHAT LOCATION TO GO TO ☸ ( ) !

HIS LOCATION GO TO **326**

DIG IN THE SAND AT THIS **TREE**

THE ISLAND OF INIALA

ADVENTURE GUIDE

"We should take the path up to the castle." Alexander was confident that the treasure would most certainly be there. "I would keep my treasure in a castle."

"The castle path it is."

The kids happily begin their adventure passing through the jungle toward the mountain trail. Emma is excited by the amazing plants and animals that she has only ever read about and Alexander is much less excited about plants. He is filled with the excitement of his new found quest and does not want to slow down to look at plants.

Both of the kids stop when they hear a rustling in the branches just off the trail. Emma is cautious and begins to move away, when she is just out of arms reach Alexander decides to investigate. He pushes back the branches and finds quite possibly the cutest, plumpest, friendliest baby elephant ever.

"Can I keep him?"

25

26

FUN FOR ALL

THEME There are two priorities in this room: Hockey (in this case, the NHL's Washington Capitals) and fun.

FOCUS The room consists of two main sections, one for kids and one for adults, and is divided by authentic hockey boards, complete with yellow kickplates and half-inch Plexiglas. Like a true hockey arena, the front half of the room pays homage to star players with two fully autographed team jerseys preserved in cases, as well as team logos positioned throughout the room on custom-made pillows, accessories and the floor. The back half of the room is made just for kids. Swings, a dart board, a ball pit, a stage and a hidden playhouse under the stairs ensure fun for all.

STORAGE A large storage unit at the rear of the room makes use of an odd-shaped nook, adds support and accommodates large shelves, toys and boxes. Storage space is cleverly placed near the ball pit, and will eventually transition into a full storage area once the pit is no longer needed. The back side of the hockey boards hold two small refrigerators (one apiece for adults and kids), as well as the base for the audio system.

GROWTH The front half of the room will last as long as the family's love for the NHL team. The back half of the room will grow with the children, and eventually will provide a useable, wide-open space as well as storage.

SAFETY A Plexiglas wall separates the two main areas of the room, minimizing the noise created by kids playing and hockey fans cheering. It also protects the big screen TV from balls, pucks and other play objects that occasionally fly by. The ball pit door has a double safety lock that requires supervised use.

Another lesson learned here: Placing a 62" TV into a hole that is 60" wide is a little bit of a problem.

— Chris Jones, Thinkterior

MODULAR PLAY WALLS

THEME The theme in this space is defined by the design and flow that characterize the family's beautiful contemporary home. The family requested that the space blend with the balance of the home while still providing the youngest family members with all the enjoyment of a dedicated playroom.

FOCUS The focus of this space changes with the configuration of the modular pieces around the room. One configuration could emphasize the television for movie night, another could create a stage for a musical performance, while a third one could close off the kids play area altogether, highlighting the importance of adult conversation. Each configuration concentrates on the activity or plans for the moment.

STORAGE Each of the modular pieces includes multiple storage options. The multimedia section ensures that all electronic equipment and remote devices have a dedicated home no matter where the section is placed. The large dedicated storage unit provides open blocks that can be filled with baskets of toys or books while creating the perfect wall in any configuration. The magnetic section showcases the display of artwork or calendars while the lower box provides closed storage and a cushioned seating area.

GROWTH These modular pieces will always be a useful and functional addition to this space, providing the family with unlimited configuration options to enable the space to evolve with the family.

SAFETY Safety is always a concern in furniture design, and modular pieces require added attention to stability and security so they will incorporate the safety of built in elements along with the desired flexibility and functionality. Custom made brackets lock the modular sections together at multiple points to keep them linked once positioned, and the rolling castors under each section also lock into place to ensure that they will not move across the floor.

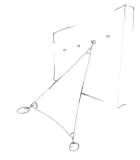

Most rooms in any home need to serve multiple functions, providing everyone in the family a space that meets their wants and needs, and that is the case with this great space. The ability to reconfigure the play area to accommodate small family nights or large play dates was as important as providing this family an area that would mature with its needs.

— Chris Jones, Thinkterior

SPORTS MOVIES GAMES

THEME This irresistible space is centered on the family's love of sports, devotion to family time, and commitment to comfortable entertaining. The room is made to relax in, to cheer on the local sports teams and to share a fun evening with friends and family. Sports memorabilia are creatively displayed along the main wall atop custom graphics proudly celebrating favorite teams. The colors, furniture and accessories selected all promote the fun-loving family's passion for entertaining and togetherness.

FOCUS The focus for this space is on flexibility. Whether the action involves watching a movie alone or hosting friends for game night, the space is effortlessly adaptable. The furniture is mounted on casters for quick and easy movement, and multiple ceiling mounts are positioned to add custom-designed seating hammocks. The television is strategically installed at a point in the room where everyone has a good view of the game.

STORAGE The family of seven has quickly put all the room's integrated storage options to good use. Discreetly hidden behind large rolling doors is a wall housing two mini refrigerators and multiple oversized baskets that easily swallow up toys, balls and games. The room also includes two custom rolling toy benches, ideal for storage and additional seating.

GROWTH The design and function of this space closely support the activities of the family. By maximizing use of the open floor plan and leveraging custom-designed, adjustable furniture, the room will retain its flexibility to serve the family for years to come.

SAFETY Each of the room's key spatial elements can be customized to so even the smallest fans can have a great time. The ceiling mounts are installed with added blocking to support both children and adults, and the casters used for all moving elements can be locked in place at the desired location.

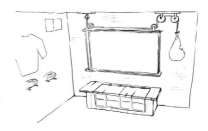

All furniture within room was fitted with wheels for easy movement for the kids in creating open play areas.

— Chris Jones, Thinkterior

FOOTBALL
BASEBALL
SOCCER
BASKETBALL
HOCKEY
DARTS >>>>>>>
MMA
LACROSSE
TEXAS HOLDEM
BLACKJACK

ARTIST PALETTE

THEME This room is dedicated to supporting and encouraging the young artist in art and music. From the hand-painted instruments decorating the music corner to the dedicated foldaway art table, every space is tailored to the creative spirit, offering a place to be inspired, a nook to relax or a corner to practice. This environment radiates energy from the ground up, showering the room in natural, vibrant color.

FOCUS A majestic, floor-to-ceiling tree anchors the space, boldly transporting the beauty of nature into the house--along with the fun of swinging from a tree branch, pitching a tent or reading under the beautiful canopy. The tree shares pride of place with a unique, retro-inspired room divider housing a colorful padded nook perfect for reading, watching television or just relaxing.

STORAGE Multiple storage options are integrated to accommodate the family's eclectic interests and varied needs. From hidden cabinets in the floor to movable shelves and storage bins, there is room for everything. The two wardrobes provide generous storage capacity without taking up valuable floor space, and readily open up to sweep toys out of sight. The myWall® panels accommodate various shelving options and bins that can all be repositioned as needed. Additional storage and display options are strategically provided around the room to store sheet music or display art projects on any of three magnetic panels.

GROWTH While the young artist experiments with media or music, he can also adapt this space to complement his experiences. The myWall® panels promote easy transformation and expansion, offer unlimited options, and keep shelving at an optimum height as he grows. All the furniture rolls on casters so the room can sustain the action during a play date or be completely re-imagined if the family wants a makeover.

SAFETY The elements in this large open space are all designed to enfold a young boy in a playful, creative and safe place. The modular components on the myWall® panels are all locked securely in place no matter what they store. The custom drop-down table includes two safety latches to prevent unintentional opening. The floor drop doors are all equipped with slow glide closing hinges so no fingers will be trapped.

Yellow rope used as hanging pulley illusion is one single length of material.

Custom bathroom French horn light was fabricated from an actual French horn.

Custom wallpaper was created for texture behind the player piano.

— Chris Jones, Thinkterior

CONTEMPORARY CLUBHOUSE

THEME The theme for this inviting and playful space is a creative take on a functional playroom joining the contemporary and functional base of the room to the playful and creative spirit of the furnishings that will engage the family's children.

FOCUS The playroom centers on a loft-like clubhouse perched on sturdy "trees," establishing the inviting feel for the room and presenting the perfect place for creative adventures or quiet reading. The playful mood continues with a custom-painted wall mural of a pasture and bright green patches of shag carpet that extend the pasture around the floor. The space is further populated with contemporary and functional elements offering endless hours of play to children ages 2-12.

STORAGE Storage options can be found on every wall, in every corner and even on the floor. On the main wall, the myWall® storage and entertainment unit offers open shelving, hanging buckets, closed shelves and pegs. The wall mural behind the clubhouse has a shelving unit portrayed as a tree in the pasture with open and closed cubbies for books or toys. The sink and craft area offers a home to all the kids' craft supplies, nestled right into the countertop with colorful containers and buckets. Even the floor under the myWall® panel is a custom "floordrobe" perfect for small floor toys or blankets.

GROWTH Though this playroom provides fun and creative options for children from 2-12, it can evolve with the children. The myWall® system promotes easy and immediate customization with simple adjustments. In fact, the full myWall® structure can be moved along with the family if necessary. The sink offers steps for the small children that can be removed when outgrown.

SAFETY The playroom is designed so the main space remains open and free of obstacles for creative and safe play. The myWall® system uses a custom locking mechanism to securely lock all elements so they will not fall or become loose from wear. Custom cushioned floor rugs offer another level of safety and comfort to the little ones playing on the floor.

The rug used had 100mm long shag, making it easy to serge the edges while still having them masked by the long shag lengths.

— Chris Jones, Thinkterior

PLAYGROUND OASIS

THEME The overall theme of the play yard is to develop a distinctive environment for creative and active outdoor play in the contemporary styling of the family's beautiful desert home.

FOCUS The overall focus for the design of the play yard is to provide a continuously adaptable outdoor space where this family can foster an active and creative playtime for their children. The visual focus of this space is the 15-foot "tree" occupying the middle of the turf yard. This fantastic structure beckons the children to climb the stairway of mini stumps and enjoy the slide or swing happily from the branches, all the while adding a natural touch of whimsy to the playground's chiefly modern-style components. Surrounding the tree is an array of play equipment for the children's activities that is incorporated in the custom myWall® system. Chalkboard walls to write and draw on, a ball wall to practice sports skills, rock climbing holds that clip into the wall, and custom water toys and games suggest some of the many possibilities the space offers.

STORAGE The myWall® system offers various storage options, including shelving, closed cases and hanging baskets.

GROWTH Since the myWall® system is meant to grow with the family, all accessories can be moved or replaced while the main frame remains in place. The playground materials have been chosen for their durability and ability to withstand harsh conditions for many years. The tree also includes three levels of swings so children of varied ages can swing from the branches.

SAFETY Safety is of critical concern with any play yard, and a space in the harsh conditions of the desert faces specific environmental concerns that our design addresses with light colors, reflecting the sun and reducing heat buildup, and stainless steel hardware, preventing corrosion. All myWall® accessories employ a locking mechanism that allows for easy adjustments, while securely locking the pieces into place.

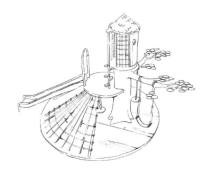

All flooring and wall materials were created with a solid core ship builder grade plastic. (regularly seen on the decks of boats)

— Chris Jones, Thinkterior

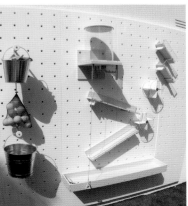

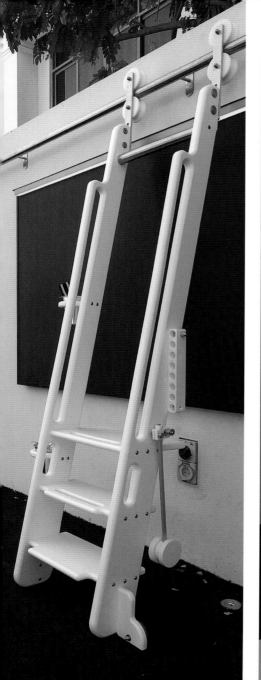

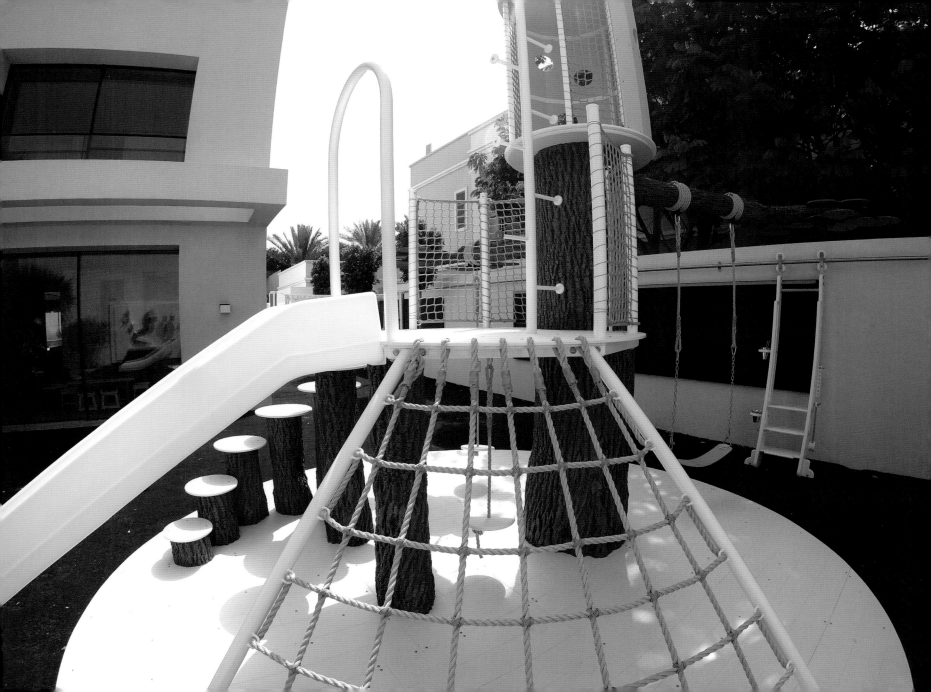

KIDS OCR

THEME The theme of this half-mile trail through the woods is evident in the fun, creative and all-inclusive obstacles hidden in the natural flow of the land around a wondrous family home. The course was created for a broad spectrum of users: adults and children, advanced and beginner athletes, and participants in competitive and entertaining events. Each of 13 obstacles is designed to be challenging yet manageable no matter who runs the course.

FOCUS The focus for this family was to create an outdoor adventure that could serve as an athletic, social and personal outlet without altering the landscape's natural beauty or the home's sweeping views. The large scale of the trail's obstacles is camouflaged by using the rolling hills and mature trees as a natural backdrop. The beauty of the course does not diminish the functional and demanding nature of the obstacles, which are designed to develop multiple strength, agility, and cardio fitness abilities and intensities.

STORAGE The start of the trail includes a raised training area offering a dedicated, aboveground storage space for bags, mats and other equipment used during the run. A small all-terrain storage cart comes with six yoga mats, three medicine balls of various weights, rings, sprinting cones, and a large digital timer to record laps.

GROWTH The course provides an athletic and fun challenge for children, teens and adults, regardless of experience or athletic prowess, to ignite their passion for physical activity. Each obstacle is paired with an instructional sign instructing participants in proper use of the obstacle, adaptations for skill levels and tips on form. The signs are customized for the course, and are printed on metal to endure.

SAFETY Safety is crucial for all physical activity, and an obstacle course of this scale presents unique safety concerns. Children should always be supervised on the course. However, meticulous care has been paid to design details to be sure everyone has a great time. All course obstacles are built with pressure treated lumber to withstand seasonal stress. All footer pilings that support obstacles have been driven into the ground between 3 to 4 feet (.9 to 1.2 meters) deep and each piling is set in concrete to guarantee the stability of the structure and the safety of the participants. Furthermore, all obstacle lumber is finished with rounded corners and finely sanded to minimize splintering and maximize enjoyment of the course.

DESIGN CONCEPTS

Every Thinkterior project is created and built in conformance with five guiding elements: Theme, Focus, Storage, Growth and Safety. These fundamental elements guide the project from inception to completion and serve as the foundation for creativity to build on.

THEME Every project has an inspiration, the core feeling or vision that the space will embody when it is complete. The theme in a Thinkterior space is not built around a single image or element, relying instead on the aggregation of details big and small to translate ideas and dreams into the perfect space for a curious child, a growing tween, or an active family. While the themes in some rooms are visually or topically specific, other spaces look to convey a feeling or attitude. Whatever the vision may be, the theme in every Thinkterior space is the organizing element of the design and fabrication.

FOCUS If the theme provides the overall look and feel of the space, there is always an element that creates a single, undeniable focal point. Whether the focus in a space is a single piece of furniture or an entire wall, it draws your attention and shapes your perception of the room, anchoring the theme and unifying the entire space. Thinkterior spaces boast some of the most creative and fantastic elements, so there may be more than one focal point in a space, but each still supports the overall theme while offering something new and exciting.

STORAGE Creativity is not limited to the artistic elements in a space. True ingenuity is found in the ability to combine practical and necessary elements with the theme's creative vision. No matter what space is being designed, storage is essential to its viability. The ability to provide innovative storage options that are seamlessly folded into the design is a key element in every Thinkterior space.

GROWTH Designing a space for a single moment in time is challenging enough, but designing a space that can unite current needs with future necessities requires creativity, ingenuity and resourcefulness rarely achieved in interior design. Designing and fabricating spaces for children and families requires an innovative approach to every project, anticipating future needs and incorporating elements that can be easily updated or changed as the needs of the family or growing children mature.

SAFTEY The wellbeing and security of every occupant in the space is a core component in every Thinkterior design, from inception and fabrication to installation. Every element or detail is reviewed and evaluated to ensure a safe environment. Thinkterior's inspired and whimsical spaces are created to enhance and support a child's imagination at the same time they offer safe, reliable places to play, relax and learn.

hanging light ←

Bed
Footboard

chimney

3528

4
1

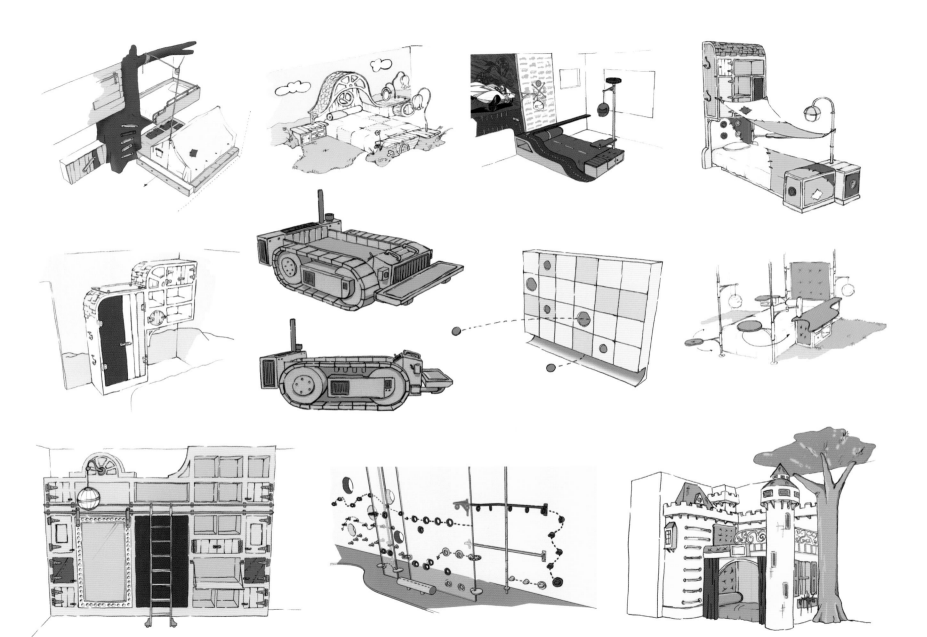

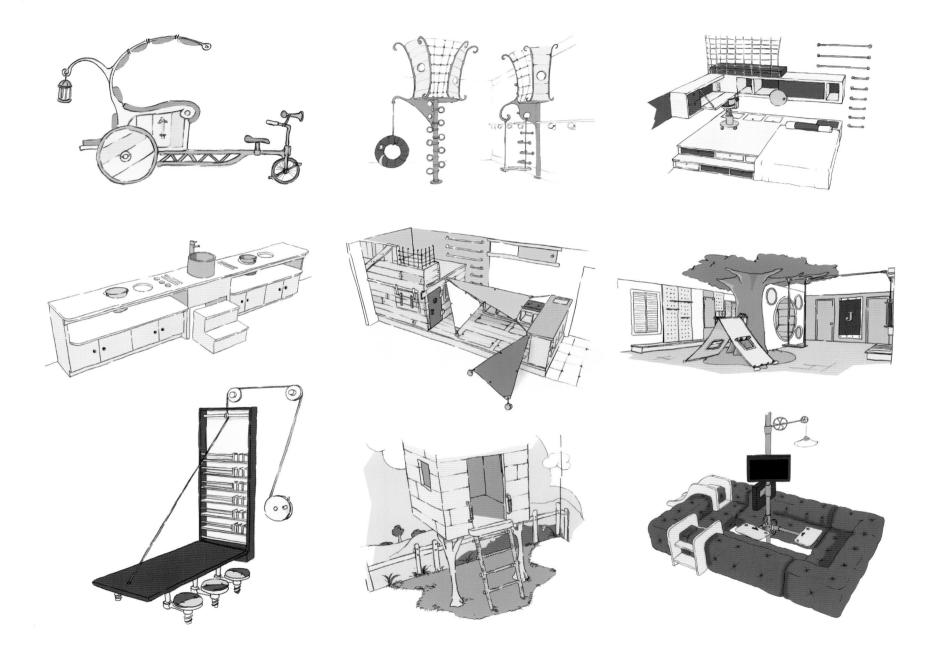

MON. 24
TUE. 25
WED. 26
THUR. 27
FRI. 28
SAT. 29
SUN. 30

NATE

toys

toys

Chris Jones
Creative Director

Cory Sokolowski
Fabricator/Artisan

Projects designed,
fabricated, or installed
worldwide.

 clients

thınkterior

Amazing Bespoke Kids Interiors

Special Thanks To

Writing:
Susan Jones
Matt Thorpe
Roger Yee

Photography:
Lucas Fladzinski
Robert Merhaut
Robert Moss
David Wiegold